i explore

SEA LIFE

Castle Street PRESS

WHAT'S INSIDE?

Discover more about the amazing world of sea life!

Fish

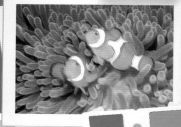

Dolphins

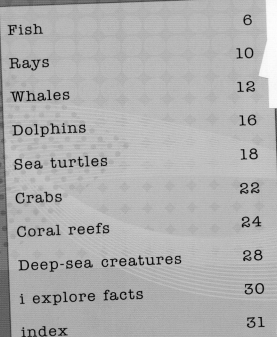

Coral reefs

Rays

Whales

Sea turtles

Crabs

Deep-sea creatures

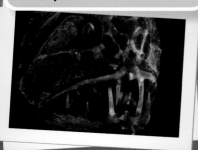

i explore facts

FISH

Despite their different shapes, sizes, and colors, most fish belong to a group of animals called bony fish, which all have skeletons made of bone.

gill cover

lipstick tang

Lionfish

mouth

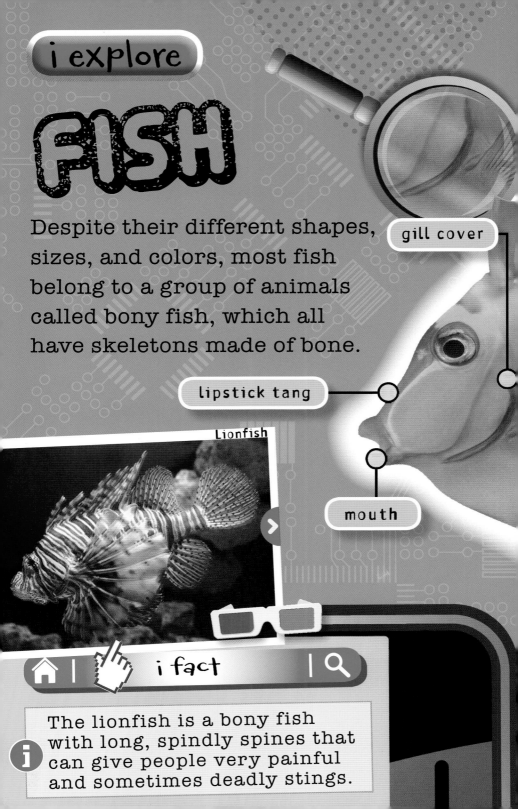

i fact

The lionfish is a bony fish with long, spindly spines that can give people very painful and sometimes deadly stings.

A fish's gills are found beneath its gill covers. A fish "breathes" by pushing water through the gills. Oxygen is taken into the fish's blood through the gills, to be carried around its body.

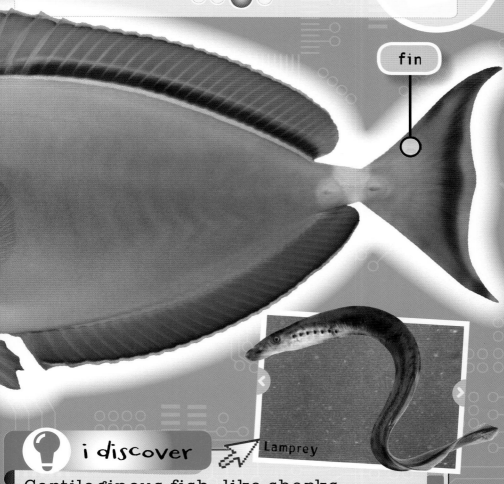

fin

i discover

Lamprey

Cartilaginous fish, like sharks, skates, and rays, have skeletons made of cartilage. Hagfish and lampreys are so unusual that they are in a group of their own called jawless fish!

Seahorse

Clownfish in a sea anemone

j Clownfish are bony fish that live in poisonous sea anemones. They are safe from the poison thanks to a coating on their skin.

Seahorses are bony fish. Male seahorses keep the eggs in a special pouch until they hatch.

RAYS

The graceful stingray has an extremely dangerous tail! At the base of its tail, a stingray has one or more venomous spines that can give people painful stings.

blue spotted stingray

→ i learn ✕

A stingray hunts along the seabed. When it catches its prey, it crushes the animal with its powerful jaws.

jaw

Underside of a stingray

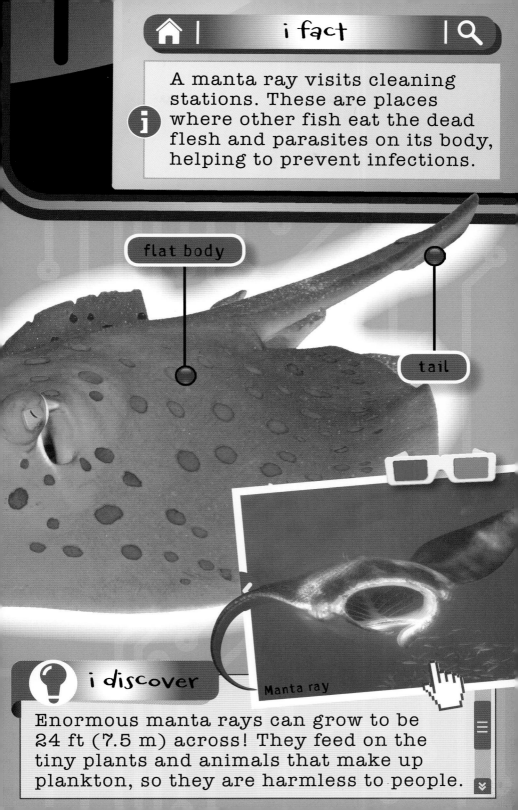

ℹ️ A manta ray visits cleaning stations. These are places where other fish eat the dead flesh and parasites on its body, helping to prevent infections.

flat body

tail

Manta ray

💡 i discover

Enormous manta rays can grow to be 24 ft (7.5 m) across! They feed on the tiny plants and animals that make up plankton, so they are harmless to people.

WHALES

Whales are marine mammals that must come to the surface to breathe. There are two different types of whales: toothed whales, like beluga whales and dolphins, and baleen whales, like the humpback!

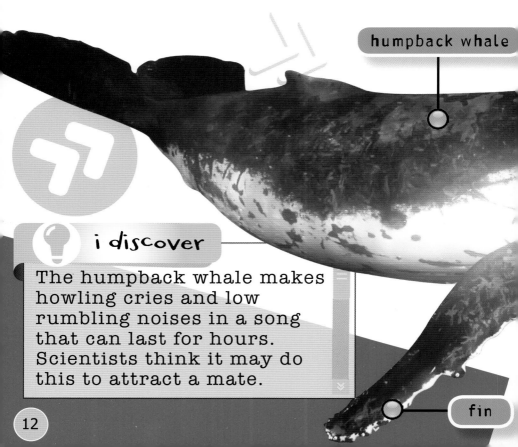

humpback whale

i discover

The humpback whale makes howling cries and low rumbling noises in a song that can last for hours. Scientists think it may do this to attract a mate.

fin

The beluga whale makes clicking and chirping noises so often that it is nicknamed the sea canary.

Beluga whale

baleen

i learn

Humpback whales sieve out food from the water with long plates of baleen. Baleen are bristles made out of the same material as human hair. Small fish and plankton are trapped in the baleen and swallowed.

ⓘ Humpback whales can jump out of the water at speeds of 18 mph (29 kph). This is called breaching.

DOLPHINS

Intelligent dolphins travel and hunt in groups called pods. It is thought that a pod will work together to help an injured dolphin to the surface of the water so it can breathe.

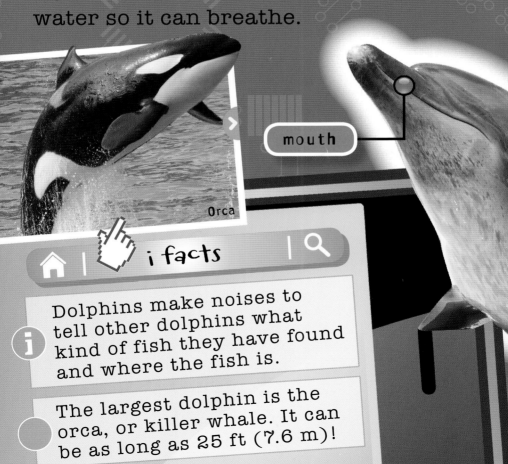

Orca

mouth

i facts

Dolphins make noises to tell other dolphins what kind of fish they have found and where the fish is.

The largest dolphin is the orca, or killer whale. It can be as long as 25 ft (7.6 m)!

The speedy bottlenose dolphin is known for its acrobatics. It can jump as high as 23 ft (7 m) out of the water and somersault before splashing back into the sea!

Bottlenose dolphins

tail

fin

➡ i learn

To hunt their prey, dolphins make a clicking noise that travels through the water and bounces off an object. The noise that echoes back tells the dolphin the size, shape, and location of the object.

SEA TURTLES

Using their strong flippers, sea turtles travel a long way to find food and to mate. Sadly, they are often caught in nets or struck by boats, so much so that sea turtles are at risk of dying out completely.

carapace

plastron

→ i learn

A sea turtle has a tough shell to protect its body from an attacker's teeth and claws. The top of the shell is called the carapace. The bottom of the shell is called the plastron.

i Sea turtles can look like they are crying, but this doesn't mean they are sad! They cry large tears to get rid of salt from their bodies.

Sea turtle crying ⊗

flipper ——○

💡 i discover

Female turtles have an excellent sense of direction and will return to the beach where they hatched to lay their eggs.

≫

male turtle laying eggs ⊗

i explore MORE

i fact

Sea turtles' eggs can produce male or female turtles depending on the temperature of the nest!

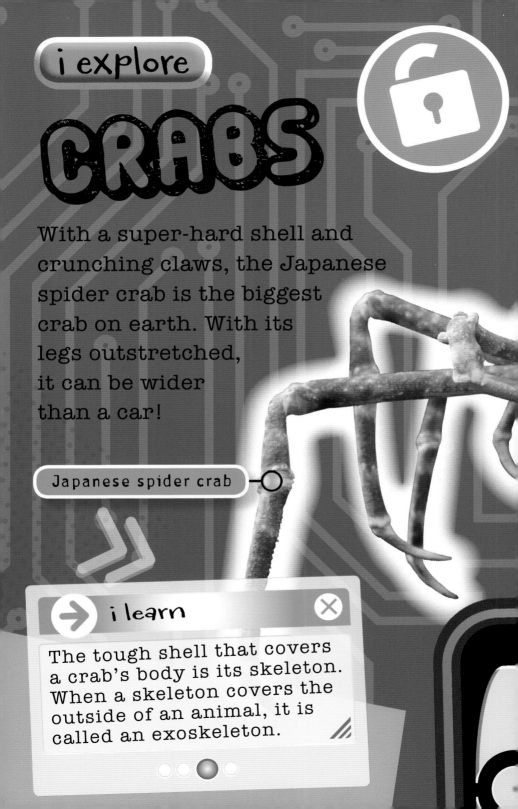

CRABS

With a super-hard shell and crunching claws, the Japanese spider crab is the biggest crab on earth. With its legs outstretched, it can be wider than a car!

Japanese spider crab ─○

→ i learn

The tough shell that covers a crab's body is its skeleton. When a skeleton covers the outside of an animal, it is called an exoskeleton.

The fiddler crab has one enormous front claw and one small one. A male fiddler crab uses its large claw to attract females and as a show of strength to other males.

Fiddler crab

shell

claw

i fact

Hermit crab

A hermit crab carries an empty shell on its back to cover its weak spot! When its shell becomes too tight, it looks for a new shell that will allow it to grow.

i explore

CORAL REEFS

Beautiful coral reefs are home to a quarter of the world's marine fish! Coral reefs are in danger from pollution, climate change, and fishing.

→ **i learn** ✕

Coral reefs are made up of large groups of small sea animals called polyps. Coral polyps are see-through – they get their beautiful colors from the simple, plant-like algae that live inside them.

Polyps

polyp

Great Barrier Reef
seen from the air

The biggest coral reef is the Great Barrier Reef in Australia. It covers an area larger than Poland!

Some of the coral reefs alive today began growing 50 million years ago!

Inside a coral reef

i explore MORE

Amazing coral reefs are home to almost 4,000 types of fish! Many fish feed on other small animals that live in the reef, while others eat the algae or seaweed on the coral. The butterfly fish uses its thin mouth to nibble at corals in search of polyps to eat.

DEEP-SEA CREATURES

Life at the bottom of the sea is tough – with little or no sunlight and extremely cold temperatures, deep-sea fish have had to develop amazing ways to survive!

esca

mouth

 i learn ✕

The anglerfish has a fleshy organ, called the esca, that sticks out of its body like a fishing rod. It uses this organ to lure its prey close enough for it to attack!

i Deep-sea fish often have large teeth to give them a better chance of catching prey in such a harsh environment.

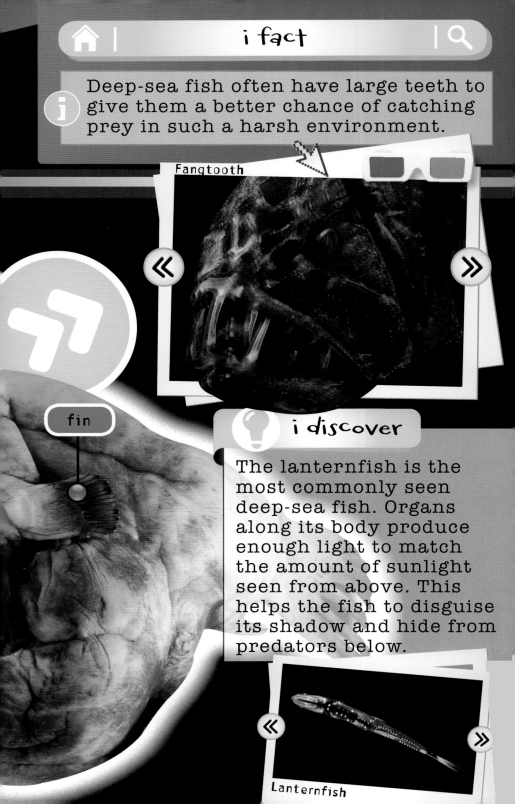

Fangtooth

«

»

fin

💡 **i discover**

The lanternfish is the most commonly seen deep-sea fish. Organs along its body produce enough light to match the amount of sunlight seen from above. This helps the fish to disguise its shadow and hide from predators below.

«   »

Lanternfish

i explore FACTS

Starfish are not actually fish – they are echinoderms, which are animals with symmetrical, pointed bodies.

Seahorses welcome each other every morning by doing a dance! This is called the morning greeting.

Some fish, like the herring, communicate by breaking wind!

Toothed whales have one blowhole, while baleen whales have two.

If a person were to dive to the deepest part of the sea unprotected, the weight of the water would crush them.

A group of fish is called a school, while a group of jellyfish is called a smack.